THE ART OF LETTING GO

POEMS ON MOVING ON AND FINDING SELF-LOVE

AF577733

UJJWAL SINGH

Copyright © Ujjwal Singh
All Rights Reserved.

This book has been self-published with all reasonable efforts taken to make the material error-free by the author. No part of this book shall be used, reproduced in any manner whatsoever without written permission from the author, except in the case of brief quotations embodied in critical articles and reviews.

The Author of this book is solely responsible and liable for its content including but not limited to the views, representations, descriptions, statements, information, opinions and references ["Content"]. The Content of this book shall not constitute or be construed or deemed to reflect the opinion or expression of the Publisher or Editor. Neither the Publisher nor Editor endorse or approve the Content of this book or guarantee the reliability, accuracy or completeness of the Content published herein and do not make any representations or warranties of any kind, express or implied, including but not limited to the implied warranties of merchantability, fitness for a particular purpose. The Publisher and Editor shall not be liable whatsoever for any errors, omissions, whether such errors or omissions result from negligence, accident, or any other cause or claims for loss or damages of any kind, including without limitation, indirect or consequential loss or damage arising out of use, inability to use, or about the reliability, accuracy or sufficiency of the information contained in this book.

Made with ♥ on the Notion Press Platform
www.notionpress.com

To anyone who has ever experienced heartbreak, this book is for you.

To the ones who have cried themselves to sleep, who have felt the ache in their chest, who have wondered if they would ever feel whole again - know that you are not alone.

This collection of poems is dedicated to those who have had the courage to love deeply, and who have had the strength to pick themselves up and start a new. May these words bring you comfort, healing, and hope for a brighter tomorrow.

And to my own personal support system - my family, friends, and loved ones - thank you for always being there to lift me up when I was down, to encourage me to keep writing, and to remind me that love is always worth the risk. I dedicate this book to you, with all my heart.

Contents

Contents

Contents

Contents

Contents

#मोहब्बत_ज़िंदाबाद

Prologue

Heartbreak is a universal experience. It is a pain that knows no bounds, a feeling that can leave us feeling lost, alone, and unsure of how to move forward. And yet, heartbreak is also a powerful force for growth and transformation.

This collection of poems is a tribute to the power of heartbreak - to the way it can break us down, and to the way it can ultimately lift us up. Each poem in this book captures a moment in time, a feeling, or an emotion that is universal to anyone who has ever loved and lost.

Some of these poems were written in the depths of heartbreak, when the pain felt all-consuming and the future uncertain. Others were written after the healing had begun, as a way to reflect on the journey and find hope for the future.

But all of them were written with the intention of offering comfort, healing, and hope to anyone who has ever experienced heartbreak. Because while heartbreak can be painful, it can also be a catalyst for growth and transformation.

My hope is that these poems will serve as a reminder that healing is possible, that love is always worth the risk, and that there is always hope for a brighter tomorrow.

Foreword

Heartbreak is a deeply personal experience, yet it is one that we all share in some way or another. It is an experience that can leave us feeling lost, alone, and unsure of how to move forward. That is why I am honored to introduce this collection of moving on poems.

In this book, you will find words that speak to the rawness of heartbreak, the process of healing, and the hope of finding love once again. Each poem captures a moment in time, a feeling, or an emotion that is universal to anyone who has ever loved and lost.

What I love most about these poems is the way they offer comfort and support to anyone going through heartbreak. They remind us that we are not alone in our pain, and that there is always hope for a brighter tomorrow.

The author has poured her heart and soul into this book, and it shows in the beauty and depth of each poem. Her words are a testament to the power of love, and the resilience of the human spirit.

So whether you are in the midst of heartbreak, or simply seeking words of inspiration and hope, I invite you to dive into this collection of moving on poems. May these words bring you comfort, healing, and the courage to keep moving forward.

With love and hope,

Ujjwal Singh

Preface

When I first started writing these poems, I was in the midst of my own heartbreak. I felt lost, alone, and unsure of how to move forward. But as I began to put my thoughts and feelings onto paper, something incredible happened - I began to heal.

Through the act of writing, I found a way to process my emotions, to make sense of the pain, and to find hope for a better future. And it is my sincerest hope that this collection of poems can offer that same sense of healing and hope to anyone who reads them.

Each poem in this book was written with the intention of capturing a specific emotion or moment in time. Some of the poems were written in the midst of heartbreak, while others were written after the healing had begun. But all of them were written with the hope of offering comfort, inspiration, and a sense of connection to anyone who has ever loved and lost.

With love and hope,

Ujjwal Singh

Acknowledgements

I am incredibly grateful for the many people who supported me throughout the writing of this book. First and foremost, I want to thank my family, who have always been my biggest cheerleaders and who encouraged me to pursue my passion for writing.

I also want to thank my friends, who provided unwavering support and encouragement throughout the writing process. Your kind words, thoughtful feedback, and encouragement kept me going when I needed it most.

And to anyone who has ever experienced heartbreak, know that you are not alone. May these poems offer you comfort, healing, and the hope of a brighter tomorrow.

With love and gratitude,

Ujjwal Singh

Chapter1

Letting go is hard to do
But it's necessary too
For when you hold on tight
You keep your heart in a fight

Chapter2

My heart is broken
But I won't be a token
Of your love that's gone
I'll pick myself up and move on

Chapter3

Memories of us still linger
But they no longer have to trigger
My heart to ache and pine
It's time to leave them behind

Chapter4

The pain of our love's demise
Fills me with tears and sighs
But I won't let it hold me down
I'll rise and wear my victory crown

Chapter5

The road ahead may be bumpy
But I'll keep moving, never stumpy
For I know that love awaits
And I'll find it without any debates

Chapter6

The past is now a memory
And though it's tough to carry
I'll keep my head up high
And bid farewell to a love that's night

Chapter7

A broken heart can be mended
But only if the past is ended
I'll take my time and heal
And with love, my soul I'll seal

Chapter8

You were once my sun and moon
But now, I'll find a new tune
One that sings of hope and joy
For love will never destroy

Chapter9

Our love was beautiful and true
But it's time to bid it adieu
For I know that there's a better one
And with time, it will come.

Chapter10

My heart was shattered into pieces
But slowly, it heals and releases
The pain that once consumed me whole
Now a memory that I can console

Chapter11

Love is a journey, not a destination
And though we had a sweet sensation
Our paths diverged, and we must part
But I'll keep walking with a strong heart

Chapter12

It's hard to let go of what we had
But it's necessary to be glad
For what we shared was once true
And now it's time to start a new

Chapter13

Time heals all wounds, they say
And though it feels like a delay
I'll trust in the process and move on
For love's journey is never done

Chapter14

The pain of goodbye can be tough
But it's better than holding on, rough
I'll cherish the memories we made
And let go of the ones that weighed

Chapter15

Sometimes, love is not enough
And though it may be rough
I'll keep the lessons we learned
And with them, my heart will burn

Chapter16

The future holds many doors
And though I'm scared of what's in the store
I'll walk with hope in my heart
And let love play its part

Chapter17

We had a love that was once true
But now, it's time to say adieu
I'll let go of the pain and tears
And welcome a future without fears

Chapter18

The pain of a broken heart may sting
But I'll spread my wings and take wing
For there's a love that's waiting for me
And with open arms, I'll let it be

Chapter19

Goodbye is never easy to say
But sometimes, it's the only way
To let go of what's holding us back
And start a journey that's back on track

Chapter20

Love can be a beautiful thing
But it can also make our hearts sing
With pain and sorrow, tears and fears
But it's worth it when love appears

Chapter21

Our love story has come to an end
But that doesn't mean we can't be friends
I'll cherish the moments we shared
And know that love is always there

Chapter22

It's hard to say goodbye to what we had
But I know that I'll be glad
For the lessons, we learned and the memories we made
And the love that we shared, that won't fade

Chapter23

The pain of a broken heart may linger
But I'll hold on to hope, not a finger
For there's a love that's waiting for me
And with open arms, I'll let it be

Chapter24

I'll keep moving forward with a strong heart
For I know that love will play its part
In my life, and in my heart
And with time, new love will start

Chapter25

Chapter26

The past is gone, and though it may hurt
I'll look towards the future, and not revert
For there's a love that's waiting for me
And with open arms, I'll let it be

Chapter27

The road ahead may be bumpy
But I'll keep moving, never lumpy
For I know that love awaits
And I'll find it without any debates

Chapter28

Our love was once a flame
But now, it's time to play a different game
I'll let go of the past and move on
And with hope in my heart, I'll dawn

Chapter29

Love may be fragile, but it's also strong
And though we've been apart for so long
I'll hold on to the hope that we'll find
A love that's true and one of a kind

Chapter30

The pain of a broken heart may linger
But I'll find the strength to use my finger
To type a message or make a call
And reach out to friends who won't let me fall

Chapter31

Goodbye may be hard to say
But it's necessary to find a new way
To let go of what's holding us back
And start a new with a new love track

Chapter32

Love is a journey with twists and turns
And though our love story may have adjourned
I'll keep walking with a strong heart
And let love play its part

Chapter33

Memories of our love will always remain
And though it may cause some pain
I'll keep them close, and with them,
I'll learn To love again, and not to burn

Chapter34

Moving on from a break-up can be tough
But with time, I know I'll be enough
To love again, and to find
A love that's true and one of a kind

Chapter35

I'll let go of the past and move on
And with hope in my heart,
I'll dawn A new day, a new start
And let love play its part

Chapter36

Love can be a beautiful thing
And though it may cause some sting
I'll keep searching for a love that's true
And with time, it will come into view

Chapter37

Our love story may be over
But I'll keep moving forward, never a rover
For I know that love will find me again
And with open arms, I'll let it i

Chapter38

It's okay to take your time to heal
And though the pain may feel like steel
With patience and perseverance,
I'll find A love that's true and one of a kind

Chapter39

Our love story may have come to an end
But that doesn't mean I won't mend For with time,
I'll find the strength to move on
And find a love that will never be gone

Chapter40

Goodbye may be hard to say
But it's necessary to find a new way
To love again and to find
A love that's true and one of a kind

Chapter41

The pain of a broken heart may last
But with hope, it will soon pass
And with time, a new love will start
And fill the void in my heart

Chapter42

I'll let go of the memories that bring pain
And hold on to the ones that make me sane
For with time, I know I'll heal
And a new love will be revealed

Chapter43

I'll cherish the moments we shared
And though our love story may have fared
I'll hold on to the hope that someday
A new love will come my wa

Chapter44

Moving on from a breakup may be hard
But with hope, I'll find a new card
To play in the game of love
And find a new love from above

Chapter45

The future holds many possibilities
And though the past may bring some hostilities
I'll keep moving forward with a strong heart
And let love play its part

Chapter46

I'll take my time to heal and grow
And though it may feel slow
With patience and perseverance,
I'll find A love that's true and one of a kind

Chapter47

Our love may have ended, but I'll keep
Moving forward and not let it seep
Into my future, for with hope and love
A new beginning will soon rise above

Chapter48

It's time to say goodbye to the past
And move on, for love will last
With time and patience,
I'll find A love that's true and one of a kind

Chapter49

The pain of a broken heart may linger
But I'll keep moving forward with vigor
For with hope and love,
I'll find A new love that will forever bind

Chapter50

I'll let go of the memories that bring pain
And hold on to the ones that will sustain
My heart in the journey ahead
And lead me to a new love that's not dead

Chapter51

Love may have caused some hurt and strife
But I won't let it define my life
For with time, I'll find the strength to heal
And a new love that will never steal

Chapter52

Moving on from a break-up can be tough
But with the right mindset and stuff
I'll find a new love that will be
The missing piece to complete me

Chapter53

Love is a journey that may have ups and downs
But with time, I'll find a love that astounds
My heart and soul and never fades
For a love like that, my heart has always craved

Chapter54

I'll keep walking on this path of love
And not let the past hinder my shove
Toward a new love that will be
The key to unlocking my heart and setting it free

Chapter55

Goodbye may be hard to say
But it's necessary to find a new way
To love again and let go of the pain
And with time, a new love will remain

Chapter56

Our love story may have ended, but I'll keep
Moving forward and not let it creep
Into my heart and soul, for with time
A new love will be born, pure and sublime

Chapter57

I'll let go of the past and start anew
For with hope and love, my heart will renew
And find a love that's true and divine
A love that will forever shine

Chapter58

It's time to let go of the pain
And open my heart to love again
For with time and an open mind
A new love I will soon find

Chapter59

I'll keep moving forward, step by step
And not let the past my heart intercept
For with hope and love,
I'll find A new love that will forever bind

Chapter60

The wounds of a broken heart may be deep
But with time, they'll slowly heal and sleep
And a new love will soon awaken
My heart to a love that's not mistaken

Chapter61

Love may have caused some hurt and strife
But it's a journey that will lead to new life
And with patience and perseverance,
I'll find A new love that will be one of a kind

Chapter62

I'll keep the memories that bring joy
And let go of the ones that destroy
My heart and soul, for with time
A new love will come and shine

Chapter63

Moving on from a break-up may be hard
But with hope and love, I'll find a new card
To play in the game of love
And find a new love from above

Chapter64

I'll embrace the journey ahead
And not let the past fill me with dread
For with hope and love,
I'll find A new love that will forever bind

Chapter65

Goodbye may be bittersweet
But it's necessary for a new love to meet
My heart and soul, and with time
A new love will be born, pure and sublime

Chapter66

I'll keep moving forward, with my head held high
And not let the past bring tears to my eyes
For with hope and love,
I'll find A new love that will forever bind

Chapter67

The scars of a broken heart may be visible
But with time, they'll become invincible
And a new love will soon ignite
My heart with a flame that's bright

Chapter68

Love may have caused some pain
But it's a journey that will lead to gain
And with patience and perseverance,
I'll find A new love that will forever shine

Chapter69

I'll let go of the past and embrace the future
For with hope and love, my heart will nurture
A new love that will be pure and true
A love that will forever renew

Chapter70

Moving on from a break-up may be tough
But with hope and love, I'll find enough
Strength to keep moving forward and never give up
For a new love that's not abrupt

Chapter71

The road ahead may be long and winding
But with time, I'll find a love that's binding
My heart and soul, and never fades
For a love like that, my heart has always craved

Chapter72

I'll keep my heart open to love
And not let the pain take over and shove
My heart away from a new love that awaits
For a love that's pure and never fades

Chapter73

I'll say goodbye to the past with a smile
For a new love is waiting for me to compile
My heart and soul and bring to life
A love that's pure and one of a kind

Chapter74

I'll take a chance on love once again
And not let the past be a hindrance or a pain
For with hope and love, I'll find
A new love that's forever kind

Chapter75

I'll keep the memories that bring happiness
And let go of the ones that cause distress
For with time and an open mind
A new love I will soon find

Chapter76

I'll let go of the pain and hurt
And open my heart to love and flirt
For with hope and love,
I'll find A new love that's always kind

Chapter77

The memories of the past may linger
But with time, they'll become smaller and thinner
And a new love will soon appear
To wash away the tears and fear

Chapter78

Love may have caused some sorrow
But with hope and love, there's a new tomorrow
And with patience and perseverance,
I'll find A new love that's always kind

Chapter79

I'll take the lessons from the past
And use them to make a love that lasts
For with hope and love, my heart will find
A new love that's pure and divine

Chapter80

Moving on from a break-up may be daunting
But with hope and love, my heart is wanting
A new love that's pure and true
A love that's meant for me and you

Chapter81

I'll keep the memories that bring a smile
And let go of the ones that are vile
For with hope and love, I'll find
A new love that's always kind

Chapter82

I'll trust that fate will guide me right
And bring me a love that's shining bright
For with patience and perseverance, I'll find
A new love that's forever kind

Chapter83

I'll say goodbye to the past with grace
And welcome a new love to take its place
For with hope and love, my heart will find
A new love that's pure and divine

Chapter84

I'll keep my heart open to love once more
And not let the past leave me sore
For with hope and love, I'll find
A new love that's forever kind

Chapter85

I'll embrace the journey of healing and growth
And trust that love will lead me both
To a new love that's pure and true
A love that's meant for me and you

Chapter86

I'll take the pain and turn it into strength
And use it to create a new love at length
For with hope and love, my heart will find
A new love that's pure and kind

Chapter87

I'll let go of the hurt and tears
And open my heart to new love and cheers
For with hope and love, I'll find
A new love that's pure and divine

Chapter88

The memories of the past may stay
But with time, they'll fade away
And a new love will soon arrive
To make my heart feel alive

Chapter89

I'll trust that love will come my way
And brighten my life every day
For with hope and love, I'll find
A new love that's one of a kind

Chapter90

Moving on from a break-up may be hard
But with hope and love, I'll find a new start
And a new love that will bring
Joy, laughter, and everything

Chapter91

I'll let go of the past with ease
And embrace a new love with a heart that's free
For with hope and love, I'll find
A new love that's pure and kind

Chapter92

I'll keep my heart open to love once again
And trust that a new love is waiting to begin
For with hope and love, I'll find
A new love that's pure and divine

Chapter93

I'll take a chance on love once more
And not let the past hold me back anymore
For with hope and love, I'll find
A new love that's pure and kind

Chapter94

I'll trust that love will find its way
And bring a new love that will stay
For with hope and love, I'll find
A new love that's pure and kind

Chapter95

The wounds of heartbreak run so deep,
But time has a way of healing.
Slowly, steadily, the pain begins to ease,
And a new day dawns with a brighter feeling.

Chapter96

The memories of you still linger on,
In every corner of my heart and mind.
But I know I must let you go,
And leave the past behind.

Chapter97

It's hard to move on when love is lost,
When all you want is to turn back time.
But sometimes the only way to find peace,
Is to leave the past behind.

Chapter98

There is a beauty in letting go,
In surrendering to what is meant to be.
For in the letting go, we find a freedom,
That allows us to truly be free.

Chapter99

The ache of heartbreak may never fully go away,
But with time, it becomes a distant memory.
And in its place, a new love may blossom,
Bringing with it a sense of possibility.

Chapter100

Love can be a cruel and fickle thing,
A force that we cannot fully control.
But even in its darkest moments,
It can also be a source of great beauty and growth.

Chapter101

I thought that love was everything,
That without it, life was incomplete.
But now I see that there is so much more,
A world of possibility waiting at my feet.

I hope these poems help you move on from your break-up. Remember that healing takes time, but with patience and perseverance, you will find love and happiness once again.

Notes

Notes

About The Author

Ujjwal Singh

Ujjwal Singh aka Theujsi is a writer and storyteller who has been captivating audiences with his unique perspectives and captivating prose. With a passion for writing from a young age, Ujjwal has honed his craft over the years and has emerged as one of the most promising voices in the literary world today.

Born and raised in India, Ujjwal has always been fascinated by the power of storytelling. He believes that words have the ability to transport readers to other worlds, to evoke strong emotions, and to inspire change. These beliefs have driven him to pursue a career as a writer, and he has been writing stories that captivate and inspire readers ever since.

Ujjwal has a keen eye for detail and a talent for weaving together different threads to create a seamless and engaging narrative. He is known for his vivid descriptions, complex characters, and thought-provoking themes. His writing is both entertaining and thought-provoking, and his readers are drawn in by his unique perspectives and insightful commentary.

Ujjwal is currently working on his latest novel, and he is dedicated to continuing to grow as a writer and exploring new frontiers in the world of literature. Whether you're a fan of fiction or non-fiction, Ujjwal's writing is sure to captivate and inspire you. So why wait? Pick up one of his books today and experience the magic of Ujjwal Singh's writing for yourself!

Let's connect through socials:

Instagram: @theujsi

Twitter: @theujsi

Facebook: https://www.facebook.com/theujsi

Email: connect@theujsi.me

Website: https://theujsi.me

#मोहब्बत_ज़िंदाबाद

Printed by Libri Plureos GmbH in Hamburg, Germany